Skyward Ballet
A Symphony of the Soul

Teri Dourmashkin Ed.D

and

Mina Carroll

Skyward Ballet

Teri Dourmashkin and Mina Carroll

Published by Teri Dourmashkin, 2024.

While every precaution has been taken in the preparation of this book, the publisher assumes no responsibility for errors or omissions, or for damages resulting from the use of the information contained herein.

SKYWARD BALLET

First edition. March 20, 2024.

Copyright © 2024 Teri Dourmashkin and Mina Carroll.

ISBN: 979-8224310616

Written by Teri Dourmashkin and Mina Carroll.

Table of Contents

To the invisible threads that weave the tapestry of friendship, binding souls across time and space. This collection stands as a testament to the unspoken words and shared silences, the laughter that echoes through the years, and the tears that have watered the gardens of our hearts. May it remind every reader of the beauty and strength found in the connections we cherish the most.

About Mina Carroll

In the quietude of her cottage, surrounded by the silent tales of her feline companions, Mina Carroll pens poetry that transcends time. An immortal spirit whose journey began in 1864, she has witnessed the world's myriad transformations, from the gas-lit streets of Victorian England to the digital glow of the modern age. Mina's verses serve as portals to past eras, blending historical insight with the timeless emotions of the human heart. A self-described cat lady, her solitude is her sanctuary, a place where the whispers of the ages converge into a symphony of words. Mina's poetry invites readers to glimpse the eternal through the eyes of someone who has lived it, offering a connection that defies the constraints of time.

https://twitter.com/CarrollMin82867

About Teri Dourmashkin

Dr. Teri Dourmashkin is a creator of worlds both tangible and intangible. As the visionary behind a line of meticulously crafted minimalist skincare products, she brings the same precision and passion to her poetry. Teri's verses are infused with a profound understanding of the human condition, reflecting the beauty and simplicity found in nature and the depths of our souls. Her work is an exploration of love, loss, and the luminous moments of clarity that define our lives. With a doctorate that speaks to her dedication and a poetic voice that reveals her heart, Teri invites readers to find solace and inspiration in her words. Her poetry, like her skincare creations, is a testament to the belief that true beauty lies in simplicity and authenticity.

https://twitter.com/TeriLoveSkin

Dancing on a bed or leaves,
My toes bared naked, my heart carefree.
My mind is in the heavens, sweet stories I weave.
You come to my dreams; shackles set free.
Wrap me in slumber, you never deceive.
Your love is sublime, I can finally breathe.

(TERI)

The seaside,
candy floss,
99's ghost train,
sugar loaf mountain,
smell of seaweed and salt air,
little row boats miles out,
sea gulls' overhead,
that summer sun warm,
and bright childhood memories are made of these.

(MINA)

Sadness takes hold, dark clouds never win.
Another impinges right through my skin.
My stomach is turning, high tides rolling in.
I walk in uncertainty, hard battles, no kin.
My life on hold, weary doll pierced with pins.
I pray to the Gods, the answers within.

(TERI)

Mesmerized by a half-remembered memory,
a dancing flame that casts a light,
that brings to life the whisper of a long-forgotten feeling,
somewhere that a life stepped of its given path,
and took the darker one instead.

(MINA)

The soul is eternal, energy never dies.
The Divine within you spanning lifetimes.
A beloved pass, bouquets endless cries.
Float through the veil, back "home," it's their time.
Such blessed peace, no deceptions, no lies.
Illusions just melt, clear visions refined.
A surge of pure love, such joy, so sublime.

(TERI)

I weighted my heart against a feather and the feather only sank,
and my heart rose higher to that place so rarefied, clear,
and bright, you did that,
you caused our love to break the laws of physics,
you turned my life upside down,
and with a kiss turned it upside down again.

(MINA)

Been hurt like sharp bends in a winding road.
But you are different, a world never known.
You feed me your love, it grows, and it grows.
I melt into dew drops, my face all a glow.
You are with me in spirit when I feel all alone.
I want to grow old with you, silky soft snow.

(TERI)

Tracing the landscape of your hand,
the blue lines of force that feed your tapered fingers,
knuckles and joints covered in rough skin, the many
imperfections that aren't imperfections at all,
but what I love about you.

(MINA).

Such stillness in waters, starlight in my hair.
Wrapped in the galaxies, nary a care.
I think of your heart so tender and rare.
I want you to hold me, as close as night air.
Unzip my mind, all my passions live there.
Lay down beside me, souls naked and bare.

(TERI)

I pushed loose strands of hair from your eyes,
and lay my forehead against yours, our breaths entwined,
a hunger overcame me,
to have one kiss from those lips that spoke such words of love.
And if this is all we'll ever have it will be enough.

(MINA)

I close my eyes; I feel the world quake.
A smile on my face, let go of the stress.
I think of you, your love makes me ache.
I waited for you a million breaths.
Kiss me beneath a thousand suns.
Tousle my hair, make me undone.

(TERI)

You ran through empty rooms trailing ghosts behind.
Bare feet on cold bare boards
And an early morning chill that reached you to the bone.
And all throughout this quiet of quietest quiets,
A voice was heard to faintly say,
Remember that upon a time I did love thee.

(MINA)

If I could see beyond this time.
I'd let go of anxiety, grey jittery mist.
I'd sit in the stillness, sing out sweet rhymes.
Patience surrounds me, not tears, and a kiss.
Self-love floating azure oceans sublime.
Soft whispers echo such beautiful twists

(TERI)

And this little piece of paradise we found,
Stumbled upon, had never thought to find,
Surrounded by a world that would have us drowned.
And you are the loadstone of my heart, and I am yours.
And we sail our own course,
We renegade sailors, we explorers of the heart

(MINA)

Gaze into the invisible veil,
Therein lies the answers, let go of the fears,
Jigsaw puzzles, perfectly fit just exhale.
Hidden reasons, release frozen tears.
Secrets of life, so much to reveal.

(TERI)

Smashed to smithereens,
A million little thoughts spread across the universe,
Letting go, falling backwards into what,
Nothingness, sweet nothingness.
Sleepy, forget nothingness

(MINA)

Love's cocoon, two souls breathe as one.
Emersed in each other, softest silk has been spun.
Some things sneak upon us, such treasures we've won.
May our hearts be eternally blessed by the sun.

(TERI)

High up, somewhere above the pain.
Just me, and the bracing night air.
And the cold stars, and the way, way below.
My life, I could fit in the palm of my hand.

(MINA)

Love does not need to be fought.
When pure intention will light up a torch.

(TERI)

Love can be dangerous,
A rush to the head,
A rush to the ground,
Standing on the precipice,
And letting go.

(Mina)

I look at the ocean so vast and wide.
My mind transfixed, another place and time.
My ears filled with music, sweet oceans tide.
I close my eyes, honeysuckles on a vine.
Dreams fulfilled or steep mountains to climb.
I manifest my desires, forever sublime.

(TERI)

Sleep in my garden dear one,
This was yours once.
Every nook and cranny you did explore.
Every sunny day in some favored spot.
You whiled away the time away.
Every single inch you knew and loved, in your own way.
And now you sleep beneath the laurel bush as peace.

(MINA)

May I lay my head upon your lap?
Read me some poetry, I cuddle and coo.
Fingers graze my hair, golden gift wrap.
Come paint my toenails, sweet honey dew.
Come wash my hair, I'm free, never trapped.
Expressions of love melt my heart, yes, it's true.

(TERI)

An angel hunkered down.
On a rooftop high above the town.
Their wings smelled of dust, earth, and time.
With piercing blue eyes, they watched the world below.
Then rising upon that spot,
They shook their wings in great violent arcs.
And pushed themselves skywards.

(MINA)

I wish it would rain torrents of love,
I wish hate would wither, sweet sacred doves,
I wish every soul mirrored heaven above.
I wish every hand would fit like a glove.

(TERI)

Standing so still, holding breath, and listening.
Always listening, always listening,
For what I don't know,
Something magical, something wonderful,
I look to the stary sky,
I look to the yellow moon,
And think beneath all this time,
Just out of grasp, there is the truth.
There is an answer.

(MINA).

Wipe out the hate, not up for debate,
Hearts full of scorn, shredded and torn.
Souls tinged with black, reclaim your fate.
Release the rage, let love be reborn.
Kindness is everything, don't let us wait.

(TERI)

My poems must rhyme without a doubt,
Mismatched words, I'll kick them out.
The lines of verse must make one smile.
And even when sad,
I'll make you glad you read my poem.
Till it stopped on this spot.

(MINA)

I turn and I twist in the cold barren air.
Darkness of midnight calls out my name.
I struggle, I plead, thick haunted despair.
How did I get here, churning old shame?
I feel all alone, silent shadows don't care.
I'll fight till I die, it's me I'll reclaim.

(TERI)

I'm smiling now, I've had my tea.
I was so down, but don't you see?
When I'm posting, my mood is floating.
And when I'm rhyming, my days are amazing.

(MINA)

Love with every breath of your being.
Love as if your life depended on it.
Because it does.

(TERI)

What you see is not me,
The photons that dance and bounce around me.
Play a wicked game upon your eye.
My image is but half a story.
This mirror doth reflect a lie

(MINA)

Only one that I love, and that is you.
The past broken windows, so much abuse.
Wrapped in chenille, sweet morning dew.
I toss my mistrust, hurtful triggers reduced.
Unwavering kindness, sweeping oceanic views.
I live in the moment; tender love songs seduce.

(TERI)

My mind is holding on by a thread.
A single thread, just one,
And it will not let me go.
Not yet.
Oh, what a conundrum.

(MINA)

Often obstacles stand in our way.
Feeling so unsteady, you swing, and you sway.
Such unhappiness, feeling locked in a cage.
Time can drag on, so much dismay.
Old books get torn, new chapters, new day.

(TERI)

Stone walls, cragged and moss covered.
Carved by weather, and time,
And all around green.
Green mountains, green fields, green souls.
And such a mild damp day,
The watery sun and kind.
I must be back home.

(MINA)

Sometimes things feel so unaligned.
If you feel like crying, let go, just unwind.
Droplets of sadness kiss your face.
Let them flow freely, a haven, God's grace

(TERI)

A splash of sunlight paying across the room,
Moving with the spin of the world, a thousand miles an hour
Oh, how those photons enchant me.
Concentrated spots of light.
Little gifts from Sol.
If I was as tiny as a butterfly.
I'd visit every sunlight isle.
That lies about the room.

(MINA)

Icicles dripping from your face.
What is torment, what's heartache?
Let others help you, spread love, not hate.
Reach out your hand, help another, don't wait.

(TERI)

Nosferatu, they called me once a long time ago.
When the legions fought and died in those northern forests of
Teutoburger.
I was there, sating my thirst.
And a thousand years later warm summer nights,
I hunted with a Medici through that sunken city,
That gem of the Adriatic.

(MINA)

Your words linger on me exotic perfume.
I smell them,
I taste them, love letters bloom.
I want you;
I crave you;
I am your Queen.
Wrap me in kindness,
Forever I dream.
I wait for you patiently; our day will come soon.

(TERI)

~*-'♡'-*~

I'm a bottle bobbing in the ocean.
At the mercy of the tides,
Tossed and turned by every passing wave,
But I have my solid ground,
A message deep inside of me,
It's I that play upon these seas,
They have no power over me.

(MINA)

If I were a genie, for what would I wish?
I would end world hunger, stop every war.
I would connect all hands, regardless of race.
I would stop all injustice, kisses of grace.
We are all the same, when we cut, we bleed.
Give up the tyranny, kindness in need.

(TERI)

I'm a bottle bobbing in the ocean,
At the mercy of the tides,
Tossed and turned by every passing wave,
But I have my solid ground, a message deep inside of me,
It's I that play upon these seas,
They have no power over me.

(MINA)

You slide your fingers through my hair.
I purr like a kitten, coo like a dove.
I breathe in your tenderness, floating on air.
Walk into my pain, like an angel above.
Dip into my soul, wash away the despair.
Dancing through lifetimes, my special love.

(TERI)

Kettle on the stove forgotten and boiling for the last five
minutes.
My kitchen looks like a sauna,
Windows steamed over with condensation,
It's a dull wet day out,
The lights are on and its nearly noon,
I've sat down at the kitchen table with a cup of tea,
And I'm content.

(MINA)

I am the sea water that tickles my toes.
I am majestic mountains caps of white snow.
I am the green forests, emerald gemstones.
I am the lotus blossoms that slowly unfold.
I am my enemy, my greatest foe.
We are all one, God's creations that flow.

(TERI)

Just close your eyes. and turn your face towards the sky,
can you smell the meadow flowers,
can you hear the dragon flies buzz,
can you feel the warm sun upon your face.
then you have become a traveler of that space, that inner place,
where dreamers go to dream their dreams.

(MINA)

Love is a healer.
It is right in your heart,
All you need do is open it,
Let us bring us together,
And not far apart.

(TERI)

~*-'♋'-*~

Into these enchanted woods I go,
What adventures await,
I'll take a step from this world to the other side,
Where dreams are real, and anything is possible.

(MINA)

Depression cuts deep into your core.
Some days are darker, muddy brown shores.
Emotions spiral, called the human race.
Some days the sun just lights up your face.
Keep hope alive, such wonder, such awe.
Look past black oceans, self-love to explore.

(TERI)

I see a flower,
I smell a flower, my world is full of joy.
I hear a bird that's singing sweetly,
My soul wants to fly.
The end.

(MINA)

When a loved one hurts, so do you.
Feelings run deep as the oceans floor.
Hearts intertwined: velvet flowers so blue.
Love letters sent, sending hugs let it pour.
Feeling their pain breaks your heart into two.
Your warmth, your kindness will see them through.

(TERI)

Just a drop of hope is all I need,
To get through each day.
And with everyone I meet on here,
The drops become an ocean clear.

(MINA)

When I was younger, did not love myself.
So much shame riddled my youth.
Shields all around, she hid from herself.
Didn't want anyone to know her truth.
I look at her now, such tears do I cry.
Never her shame, cast away on a shelf.
She was always beautiful, that I cannot deny.

(TERI)

And in that ancient forest on the emerald Isle,
I sat beside the campfire and contemplated the task before me.
For tomorrow I must do battle with Titania herself, queen of
the fairies.
And if I fail, my very soul is forfeit and my love is lost to me
forever.

(MINA)

I need an anchor, don't want to drown.
Swimming chilly waters, ancient frozen tears,
I have fought so hard, frigid winters, many years.
Come sing to my ears, such peaceful sounds.
I need a lifeboat, one that's called faith.
I am my own savior, must have patience and wait.

(TERI)

As the day began to fill her room, she opened her eyes.
Lying in her bed snuggled beneath her duvet,
Her mind still unfocused from a peaceful night's sleep.
Through her open window, the sounds of waking morning greet
her,
And a smile plays across her face.

(MINA)

You take me to places I never have dared.
Floating on whispers, I tingle and swoon.
Such words of love, I never have known.
My ears could hear, no remnants to share.
Such tenderness heals ancient wounds.
I soar into paradise; sun kisses the moon.

(TERI)

I don't have much time left,
but my story is nearly done.
Within these volumes is a record of what happened that fateful
day,
The day the machine was turned on,
Fool's utter fools and now it's too late,
There is no going back, what is done cannot be undone.

(MINA)

I sit and stare at the pouring rain.
I hope that my struggles have not been in vain.
Pain a gift, strange ribbons, and bows.
Digging through tunnels, let go of the woes.
I need some miracles, straight down to my toes.

(TERI)

The day winds down, the hours slowly changing their pace,
The sun dips low to the horizon, taking the blue from the sky
with it,
Physics working its magic on dust turning the world the softest
shade of orange,
The lazy laden heat of the day clinging on for a little while more.

(MINA)

I touch you; I taste you, etched into my soul.
All in my mind now, my fantasies take hold.
So vivid, so real, I feel your embrace.
Vintage black stockings, Victorian lace.
I give my heart only to you.
I've waited a lifetime, please let this be true.

(TERI)

Procrastination is not my destination.
I've had a coffee,
I've feed the cats,
I've thrown a ball to a poodle too,
And now I sit in a sunny nook,
Is this to be my fate today,
A book, some Schubert a dreamy day,
Or lift my feet and head works way.

(MINA)

I gaze at blue skies; I see your sweet eyes.
Such kindness and love, sun peeking through.
I sit in my doll house; I wait for sunrise.
I walk through the night, feelings inky dark blue.
Your soul anchors me the darkest of storms.
I trust divine timing; our lives will transform.

(TERI)

Muddy cobblestoned streets,
Wet snow chilled me to the bone.
My nose, bitten raw with cold.
Smokey lamps and candles coming to life,
In grimy shop windows,
There melancholy light filling the footpaths.
The skirts of my coat splattered with the filth of the road.
Fog coming down.

(MINA)

You drive me crazy; you make me undone.
My love for you, I crave like the sun.
I've waited for you a lifetime through.
Hand in hand, softest silk has been spun.
Floating on billowy skies azure blue.
We softly embrace, just us two.

(TERI)

Have you ever walked through a meadow of long grass on a
midsummer day,
With arms outstretched on either side,
The feel of the dry grass stalks as you scythe them with your
hands.
And the dry sweet smell all around.
And all you want to do is lie down and look at the sky.

(MINA)

Where did you come from, soft breeze in my hair?
I dance through a meadow, fragrant flowers renew.
Am I dreaming or awake, do I really care?
Never been in love until I met you.
So many years, empty boxes unglued.
Look into my eyes, do you see what I've missed?
You whisper sweet nothings, too hard to resist.

(TERI)

The play of light and shade upon the face,
The way the hair seems to glow, This is the landscape that
captures me the most,
And just three colours does the painter needs to render such a
countenance to canvas,
If God can be found anywhere it's in the human face.

(MINA)

There is nothing to say, the day slips away.
My words are bereft of meaning or depth.
My heart is sinking, just don't want to stay.
I just long to take a heavenly breath.
From hopeless to hopeful, I will find my way.

(TERI)

Did you love *Skyward Ballet*? Then you should read *Waves of Enlightenment*[1] by Teri Dourmashkin!

[2]

Dive into the enchanting world of 'Waves of Enlightenment: The Beautiful Rhythm of Words,' a mesmerizing collection of poetry.Within its pages, explore the diverse spectrum of human emotions in two captivating chapters: 'Different Shades of Love' and 'A Myriad of Feelings.'These evocative verses will transport you through the labyrinth of feelings that define our existence, offering a poignant reflection of our shared humanity.Experience the power of words to stir your soul and provoke introspection in this extraordinary poetic journey.Whether you are a seasoned

1. https://books2read.com/u/4ALRj0

2. https://books2read.com/u/4ALRj0

poetry enthusiast or someone new to the world of verse, "Waves of Enlightenment: The Beautiful Rhythm of Words" is a literary treasure that will resonate with your heart and soul. Immerse yourself in the lyrical beauty of Teri Dourmaskin's poetry and let it carry you on a journey of self-discovery, reflection, and enlightenment.

Read more at terilove.com.

Also by Teri Dourmashkin

Ripples of Serenity
Waves of Enlightenment
Elixir of Love
Love's Eternal Dance
Skyward Ballet

Watch for more at terilove.com.

Also by Mina Carroll

Skyward Ballet

About the Author

Dr. Teri Dourmashkin, Ed.D., is the founder of a minimalist skincare line, known for its natural ingredients and handcrafted batches. Alongside her skincare expertise, she is a passionate poet, blending beauty and wellness in both her professional and creative pursuits.terilove.com

Read more at terilove.com.